Actuary A... and the Future-Telling Zoo

John Lee
Illustrations by Jasmin Li

Abby Actuary and the Future-Telling Zoo
Copyright © 2023 John Lee

All rights reserved. No part of this book may be copied or reproduced in any form, except for the sample pages on John's website at ActuarialTutor.uk/books which may be shared online or in print as long as the book, author and illustrator are referenced. For all other uses, please obtain written permission from the author at ActuarialTutorUK@gmail.com.

Kingdom Collective Publishing

Unit 10936, PO Box 6945
London, W1A 6US
kingdomcollectivepublishing@gmail.com

Book cover idea by John Lee, design by Jasmin Li
Illustrations by Jasmin Li, fiverr.com/jlartist
ISBN: 978-1-912045-06-8

First Edition: December 2023

Disclaimer

The author cannot be held responsible for any trauma or mental scarring caused by children reading this book or by having it read to them.
Parents should carry out a full risk-assessment of whether the child's psyche is robust enough to withstand a book about actuaries.

Other books by the author

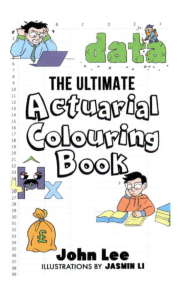
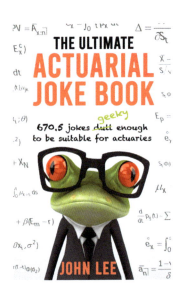

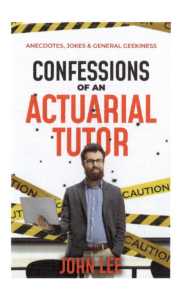

Dedication

This one's for my fabulous illustrator Jasmin.

The hours spent searching through over 100 illustrators on Fiverr was worth every moment.

Acknowledgements

I am indebted to my wife, rhymezone.com and ChatGPT for helping me to rewrite my explanations into rhyming verse.

Thanks again to my illustrator, Jasmin, for bringing these verses to life, and last but definitely not least, many thanks to my reviewers for giving their honest feedback so this book can be the best it can be:

Leigh Costanza, Emma Wang, Greg Solomon, Kanishka Singhal, Chris Grassick, Jerry Tuttle, David Yardley, CATuary (@Catuary1), Adam Biroš, Raquel Stokes, Matt Winder and Akash Malpani.

In Forecast Falls, a town not too far,
Lived Abby the Actuary, a maths superstar.
With a twinkle in her eye and a calculator in hand,
She'd predict and plan - the very best in the land.

"Join me, young explorers," she said with glee,
"To discover the secrets of an actuary!"
So every morning at the zoo door,
Children gathered — there's so much in store!

"But what's an actuary?" young Timmy cried.
"We're just like time-travellers," Abby replied.
"We peek at the past then compare with today,
And guess what's next in a math-magical way!"

"It's my zoo of tomorrow, a wonderful place,
Where all creatures of numbers have their own space.
Each one tells a story of what might just be,
That's our actuarial magic, as soon you'll see!"

At the heart of the zoo, something roared aloud!
It's the Risk-Roaring Lion, majestic and proud.
"He warns us of risks, be they big or so small,
And the wisest of actuaries take heed of his call."

"But what's a risk?" little Timmy did ask.
So Actuary Abby stepped up to the task.
"Life's an adventure, we must all hold tight,
And risk is the chance that things don't go right."

"When you ride on your bike or climb up a tree,
There's a chance that you'll fall – that's a risk, you see!
But it's not just about danger or a possible fall,
It's ALL unknown outcomes, whether big or quite small."

"But actuaries stand with the lion by their side,
Ensuring all risks are known and not left to hide.
The lion helps us choose the safest, smartest way,
So we're prepared for all, at work or at play."

"Next up," Abby pointed, "a marvellous sight!
The Probability Peacock, with feathers so bright.
With their colourful hue, each feather does show
The chance and probability, which helps us to know."

"But what is probabili-TEA?" little Timmy said.
"Is it a drink you have with jam and bread?"
"No, not a drink like coffee or tea,
But how actuaries measure risk, you see."

"In a world full of guesses some big and some small,
Probability helps us make sense of it all.
From the impossible chance that pigs might fly,
To the certain chance the sun comes up in the sky."

"From flipping a coin to the roll of some dice,
Will the weather be sunny, stormy or ice?
Each feather tells a story of what's happened before,
And actuaries count them to guess what's in store!"

In the whispering woods, where the Knowledge Trees sway,
Lived a small friendly creature, both fluffy and grey.
"Meet the Data SQuirreL," Abby said with delight,
"It sorts data nuts by day and by night."

"But what is data?" young Timmy did go,
"Data are facts that we want to know.
From the lion's risk-roar, to birthdays and weather,
And the probabilities shown by the peacock's fine feather."

"Knowledge Trees gather these facts far and wide
And store them in nuts for there to reside.
The SQuirreL SELECTs nuts FROM wherever they're found,
Sorts them into rows and INSERTs them in the ground.

"Each nut she selects, each nut she does take
Provides all the facts for decisions we make.
Actuaries rely on this squirrel so wise,
To help us plan for the future's surprise."

"But what is modelling?" Timmy wanted to know,
"Is it someone building from a box of Lego?"
"The mole builds a map of what's yet to be,
But he's using data instead of blocks, you see."

"If we want to know if tomorrow is sunny or grey,
We'd first look at the past to see what it might say.
By counting the days that were rainy or blue,
The patterns will show us what weather is due."

"So the mole studies the past to understand the trends,
Then digs time tunnels of what the future sends.
To model the future is a math-magical art,
And predicting what's coming using data is smart."

Next, Abby led them to a corner of the zoo
Where ants were busy moving in an orderly queue.
"Meet the Insure-Ants," she said with much glee,
"Who make safety nets for you and for me."

"When trouble comes knocking, be it big or quite small,
Insure-Ants are ready to answer the call.
From sickness or storms, to accidents like spills,
Insure-Ants help cover life's unexpected bills."

"But how does it work," asked Timmy that day,
"Where do the ants get the money to pay?"
"Well, each person gives an amount that's quite small,
And the ants pool it together to help one and all."

"For while many contribute to this big safety pot,
Only a few will need help, believe it or not.
By pooling together, risks are shared and spread thin
Actuaries and Modelling Mole, ensure it's a win-win."

On a nearby perch, Pension Parrot jumped out,
"Save for tomorrow!" was its squawky loud shout.
"That noisy parrot," said Abby with glee,
"Is speaking of pensions, for you and for me."

"A pension," said Timmy, "What exactly is that?"
So they both sat down to have a short chat.
"When you get older and can't work anymore,
Then retirement is what you have waiting in store."

"When those days of working are over and done,
A pension makes sure your retirement is fun.
For while you're working, you save money in a pot
So when you retire, your pension provides a lot."

"Here again, actuaries play their fabulous role:
Guiding pension funds with the Modelling Mole.
To predict, plan and give help, oh so wise,
So that pension savings grow to the right size."

In a meadow of gold, where the money flowers sprout,
The Investment Bees are working, buzzing all about.
Actuaries take money from parrot and ants' savings pot,
And they plant it all like seeds, so it will grow a lot.

"Money," said Abby, "mustn't just sit and wait.
It should grow and compound, at an awesome rate.
Soon grow the stock, bond and other money flowers,
And Investment Bees gather their coins in for hours.

But sometimes seeds don't grow as they should,
So we plant different ones, and overall we're still good.
Timmy asked, "Why plant seeds when it could go wrong?
Why not leave it in the bank no matter how long?"

"In a bank," Abby said, "money doesn't grow so fast.
So you'd have to save more, if your money's to last."
"By taking a risk, there's a greater reward.
So that much more money can easily be stored!"

Abby showed them the last animal at the zoo:
Regulation Owl, with a vital job to do.
Perched upon a branch way up so very high,
Regulation Owl keeps a constant watchful eye.

"Regulation, what's that?" asked Timmy so bold.
"These are the rules that actuaries must hold.
And the regulation owl with his eyes so bright,
Makes sure that ev'rything's done just right."

"Laws and guidelines in his talons clutched tight,
He hoots out rules from morning through to night.
For every calculation, every model that's run,
The owl makes sure that it's properly done."

"Owls like me keep the zoo true and fair,
Making sure everything is done properly with care."
Nothing's ever missed when the owl is about,
The most important role without a doubt.

With no more animals left to view,
Abby smiled and said, "Now, my tale is through.
So if someone asks you what on earth actuaries do,
Remember these creatures of the Future-Telling Zoo."

And as the day ended with the sun sinking low,
Timmy's eyes sparkled - a wonderful glow.
"To predict and to plan, with maths as your guide,
I think being an actuary must be a fun ride!"

Abby laughed and nodded, "It's true, as you say,
We make tomorrow better, by working today.
With numbers and charts, and data so neat,
Being an actuary truly is sweet!"

So in that town, not too near or too far,
Kids dreamt of becoming a maths superstar.
For in tales Abby told, one thing was so true,
With maths and some data, there's much you can do!

About the Author

John was born with his cord around his neck.
He seemed all right, but his humour was a wreck.

John studied maths & teaching at Oxford Uni,
But he still refers to himself in the third person, you see.

John's now an actuarial tutor in the UK,
But that's only what he does in the day.

He lives near Oxford with his family and wife,
And writes comedy books to make up for no life.

About the Illustrator

Jasmin is a young artist, from Toronto,
With a passion for art and dreams that flow.

Creating art that brings love, joy and laughter,
Leaving an impression that lasts ever after.

Printed in Great Britain
by Amazon